# Habeas Corpus

JILL MCDONOUGH has taught incarcerated college students through
Boston University's Prison Education Program since 1999. Her poems
have appeared in *The Threepenny Review*, *The New Republic*, and *Slate*.
The recipient of fellowships from the National Endowment for the
Arts, the Fine Arts Work Center, and the Dorothy and Lewis B.
Cullman Center for Scholars and Writers, she is currently a Wallace
Stegner Fellow at Stanford University.

WITHDRAWN

# Habeas Corpus

## Jill McDonough

SALT

CAMBRIDGE

PUBLISHED BY SALT PUBLISHING
14a High Street, Fulbourn, Cambridge CB21 5DH United Kingdom

© Jill McDonough, 2008

The right of Jill McDonough to be identified as the
author of this work has been asserted by her in accordance
with Section 77 of the Copyright, Designs and Patents Act 1988.

First published 2008

Printed and bound in the United States by Lightning Source

Typeset in Swift 9.5 / 13

ISBN 978 1 84471 472 8 hardback
ISBN 978 1 84471 424 7 paperback

Salt Publishing Ltd gratefully acknowledges
the financial assistance of Arts Council England

1  3  5  7  9  8  6  4  2

# Contents

# Acknowledgments

Grateful acknowledgment is made to the editors of publications in which the following poems first appeared:

*An Anthology of Irish-American Poetry*: "June 28, 1895: Michael McDonough" and "June 11, 2001: Timothy McVeigh"

*Fulcrum*: "October 29, 1901: Leon Czolgosz"

*Harvard Review*: "June 1, 1660: Mary Dyer" and "August 30, 1850: Professor John W. Webster"

*Literary Imagination*: "August 23, 1927: Nicola Sacco," "August 23, 1927: Bartolomeo Vanzetti," and "June 11, 2001: Timothy McVeigh"

*The Massachusetts Review*: "November 11, 1831: Nat Turner"

*Mantis*: "February 25, 1755: Tom, a Negro" and "January 17, 1977: Gary Gilmore"

*Memorious*: "June 4, 1715: Margaret Gaulacher," "October 21, 1773: Levi Ames," "July 9, 1819: Rose Butler," "June 9, 1916: Juan Sanchez," and "September 3, 2003: Paul Hill"

*The New Republic*: "February 8, 1924: Gee Jon" and "December 7, 1982: Charles Brooks"

*New Texas*: "August 9, 2000: Brian Roberson" and "August 9, 2000: Oliver Cruz"

*Notre Dame Review*: "October 8, 1789: Rachel Wall," "April 11, 1778: Aaaran," and "January 31, 1945: Private Eddie D. Slovik"

*PN Review*: "April 25, 1822: Samuel Green," "January 31, 1850: Reuben Dunbar," "December 2, 1859: John Brown," "June 19, 1863: Private William Grover," "July 7, 1865: Mary Eugenia Surratt," "November 10, 1865: Major Henry Wirz," "August 14, 1936: Rainey Bethea," "June 19, 1953:

Julius and Ethel Rosenberg," and "May 13, 2005: Michael Ross"

*Post Road*: "July 16, 1692: Susanna Martin" and "September 18, 1755: Mark and Phillis"

*Redivider*: "April 22, 1831: Charles Gibbs" and "May 2, 1960: Caryl Chessman"

*Slate*: "December 12, 1884: George Cooke"

*The Threepenny Review*: "October 22, 1659: Mary Dyer," "July 12, 1726: William Fly," "May 3, 1946: Willie Francis," and "May 9, 1947: Willie Francis"

These poems were written with the help of fellowships from the the Boston Athenaeum, the Dorothy and Lewis B. Cullman Center for Scholars and Writers at the New York Public Library, the Fine Arts Work Center, the National Endowment for the Arts, and the Virginia Historical Society.

My parents, Jim and Judy McDonough, gave me a laptop and scanner that helped me with my work in libraries at Harvard, The Boston Athenaeum, the New York Public Library, the Boston Public Library, the Virginia Historical Society, the Massachusetts Historical Society, the UMASS-Boston Massachusetts archive, and the Bancroft room at UC-Berkeley. I'd like to thank all of the librarians who helped me; Lisa Starzyk and Mary Warnement, of the Boston Athenaeum, deserve special mention for their patience, resourcefulness, and friendship.

Thanks to Mark Mazo and Mike Phipps, my research assistants, and to Harvard Extension School for providing them.

Charlotte Bacon, Eavan Boland, Todd Hearon, Major Jackson, Wendy Lesser, Gail Mazur, Jim McCue, Joseph O'Connor, Josey Packard, Robert Pinsky, Christopher Ricks, Lilly Roberts, Michael Schmidt, Billy Sothern, and Jean Strouse all provided valuable ideas and feedback.

Maggie Dietz read and commented on drafts of every sonnet here, keeping me focussed on metrical and formal rigor within the pleasures and tangents of the research.

Habeas Corpus

# Early 1608: George Kendall
*Jamestown, Virginia*

*The President did beat James Read, the Smyth.*

*The Smyth not only gave him bad language,* but soon

*stroake him againe and offred to strike him with*

his sledge, or cross peen hammer, *some of his tools.*

*The smith was by a Jury condemned to die:*

he became *pentitent,* and asked to speak

in *private.* A *dangerous conspiracy,*

he said, threatened the president—the chief

conspirator being Kendall. So Read got off,

and Kendall was brought to trial, accused of theft,

*dissension,* atheism, a mutinous plot,

*was by a Jury condened & shot to death.*


Amid *famine, fluxes, Fevers,* Kendall, betrayed,

was the first man executed by the state.

## October 22, 1659: Mary Dyer
*Boston, Massachusetts*

She walked between two men. All three bound

to be hanged, *the greatest joy and honor in*

*this world* for Quaker missionaries found

in Boston. First, she watched them hang the men,

hemp rope tossed over the limb of the elm. Then that noose

around her neck, her arms bound tight behind

her back, and Wilson's handkerchief tied loose

over her face. Her homespun skirts were tied

around her ankles after she climbed the rungs

that they had climbed. A ladder, a hanging tree.

*No eye can see, no ear can hear, no tongue*

*can speak* her willingness to die. They freed

her then, untied her, granted her reprieve:

she heard, but could not move, and would not leave.

# June 1, 1660: Mary Dyer
*Boston, Massachusetts*

Our Iphigeneia: released, alive, confused
and disappointed. Her fellow Quakers: stripped
and buried on the spot. She was hauled in a fugue
to jail, then to her son and husband. Ripped
from destiny, she lived in Rhode Island till
she came back, to show us the guilt of our blood,
and was hanged until dead from the elm on the Common. Will,
who works in the Athenaeum, shakes his head,
says *she was asking for it*. Her unmarked grave
is just outside the window, but it's still true:
*I rather chuse to Dye than to Live.* You have
*no other weapons? Wo is me for you!*
Again they bound her skirts and covered her face
in *Boston, the bitterest, darkest professing Place.*

## July 19, 1692: Susanna Martin
*Salem, Massachusetts*

She hurt Elizabeth Browne with *nayls & pinns,*

*as birds peking her legs or priking her*

*with the mosion of thayr wings,* choking her then

with *a bunch lik a pulletts egg.* She made a sure

man lose his way, *be wildered,* striking at lights

with sticks. She kept John Pressy's cowherd small

and came in Bernard Peache's window at night

to *Lay upon him an hour or 2 in all*

till he felt *loosined or lightened.* Jarvis Ring

she afflicted by *Lying upon him in bed*

or turning into a hog. She sent a thing

*like apupy* to haunt John Kimball, witnesses said.

They condemned her, for these *just and sufficient proofs,*

to the cart, and Gallows Hill, and a hempen noose.

# June 4, 1715: Margaret Gaulacher
*Boston, Massachusetts*

The news that week includes a *lyoness*

displayed, attacking *Fowls* and *Catts*. They watched

her feeding time, remarked on her *merciless*

*cruelty*. Meanwhile, Cotton Mather preached

against *Hard-hearted Sinners, Hardness of Heart*.

He helped with her confession, which reflects

on attempts to destroy her unborn child, a part

of her *Wicked* crime, completed through *Neglect*.

Now hers is a *Stony Heart, of Flint. Ah! Poor*

*Margaret, behold*: the congregation calls

for your *wondrous Industry, Agony*, your death four

days off. Pray for a *Clean, and a Soft Heart*; don't fall

from this fresh gallows to *the Mouths of Dragons*,

unconcerned, *adamant, so little broken*.

# July 12, 1726 : William Fly
*Boston, Massachusetts*


A boatswain on an English slaver, he threw

his masters overboard, was caught within

the week. In prison, he refused all food

and drink, except for rum. Refused to forgive

his enemies, or say he had: *No. I*

*won't dy with a lye in my mouth.* He swore all the way

to the scaffold, *wished the Goddamned ship would fly*

*away with devils, cursed himself, the day*

*he was born, and her that bare him,* heaven, the god

who judged him, the man who turned him in. They prayed

for his repentance. He offered scorn, then awed

the crowd with advice to the hangman on his trade:

he tied the knot himself. They let him sway,

then tarred his body, and gibbeted him in the bay.

# February 25, 1755: Tom, a Negro
*Amelia County, Virginia*

We know John Clark owned Tom, and testified
*he saw Tom have a knife in his hand, and stabb*
*William Clark with it, of which wound he died.*

Tom pled not guilty. John Clark, *Witness*, added
Tom *likewise endeavored to stabb him*. And, *he did*
*also stabb* their neighbor. Who *bled very much.*

He was sentenced to *hang by the neck till he be Dead,*
*his head severed, his Body to be cut*
*up into four Quarters. His Head to be stuck*
*up at the Cross Road near Jones's, a Quarter near*
*Wily's, one at Farley's,* one at some *publick*
*place.*

The Virginia Atlas and Gazetteer,
2000, still shows *Amelia County Courthouse,*
*Paineville, Blackman Creek, Lew Jones Road, Skin Quarter.*

## September 18, 1755: Mark and Phillis
*Cambridge, Massachusetts*

Was he your master? *Yes he was.* How did

he die? *I suppose he was poisoned.* Do you know

he was poisoned? *I do know he was poisoned.* She'd

been his for thirty years, then finally stowed

*White Powder behind a black Jug,* doctored the water.

And had your master any? *Yes he had.*

*In barly Drink, and Watergruel.* His daughters,

*Miss Betsy and Miss Molly,* served their dad.


*It was Mark who first contrived it, he had read*

*the Bible through. Laying Violent Hands*

*by sticking or stabbing or cutting his throat to shed*

*his blood's a sin.* Phillis blamed Mark on the stand

and was burned alive at the stake, while he was hanged,

his body up for years, displayed in chains.

## October 21, 1773: Levi Ames
*Boston, Massachusetts*

*My first thefts were small. A couple of eggs, and then*

*a jack-knife. After that some chalk. A fair*

*piece of broadcloth, a silver spoon and ten*

*or eleven dollars from Mr. Symond. A pair*

*of silver buckles, twelve tea-spoons, silk mitts.*


He asks the preacher for this psalm: My heart

is smitten, and withered like grass, so I forget

to eat my bread, &c. *My time is so short.*


He reads Ezekiel: A new heart will

I give you, &c. *For my heart was bad,*

*bad indeed.* At the gallows he asked if the souls

of the wicked, at death, would appear before our God

or immediately pass to Hell, and wait their doom.


*Soon, dear sir, I shall know more than you.*

## April 11, 1778: Aaaran

*San Diego Mission, California*

*Los indios de Pamo* pulled back and aimed

their flaming arrows at the tule roofs.

Their songs called priests *demonicos*, and claimed

they'd stolen land, controlled the rain. Fresh troops

arrived to guard new tile. Aaaran was bold

and unrepentant, busy trying shafts,

stockpiling clubs *por los cristanos*. He told

the soldiers "come and be slain," planned fresh attacks.

*Por insolencia, conspiradad*

four men were sentenced to public deaths. Two days

in jail, and then two bullets each. The sad

priest charged with each man's soul was told to save

Aaaran by Saturday, make him repent

and die with Christ. Or not: *y si no, tambien.*

# October 8, 1789: Rachel Wall
*Boston, Massachusetts*

The woodcut illustrating *Life, Last Words*
*and Dying* CONFESSION, *of* RACHEL WALL: a child's
dark awkward house, a ladder slanting toward
three figures, hanging above the crowd that piled
onto cobbles to watch three robbers hang,
and one a woman. The picture's clumsy. Still,
her petticoats, small bodice are portrayed
in detail. She said she never robbed that girl,
but did admit that she deserved to die:
the gold she stole from *under the captain's head,*
asleep at *Long-Wharf. Sabbath-breaking.* The lie
that got another woman whipped in her stead:

*I declare the crippled Dorothy Horn*
*innocent of the theft at Mr. Vaughn's.*

## July 8, 1797: Abraham Johnstone
*Woodbury, New Jersey*

As part of his *Dying Confession*, he wrote an *Address*
on new patriots holding slaves while they grasped
at *freedom, liberty, natural rights.* He stressed
that all his masters *loved* him. Here, in his last
hours of thought, last chance to set things right,
he recounts throwing himself between his master
and a *negro man* with a grudge and a hidden knife.

I've read a lot of these: they thank a pastor,
warn others to be good, admit some crimes —
they don't recount their best-rewarded stunts.
But Othello does it, too. Act Five: he reminds
himself, his captors, that in Aleppo once
he smote a turbaned enemy of the state.
Maybe they felt these acts were their mistakes.

# July 9, 1819: Rose Butler
*Potter's Field, New York, New York*

To be sent in a cart to State Prison, to climb the stairs

to the attic, where the women are kept, and left

there, left in that close heat with strangers, their

children, their sweaty bodies. Charged with theft,

say. Rats, fleas, cholera, buckets of shit, and years

spent fighting, trapped there, forgotten till you died.


The preacher visits her holding cell and swears

she's *sure to go to hell.* The Sheriff's kind,

gives her an orange, a ride in a coach, at last,

to the gallows. She'd dreaded a cart. They tie black bows

at her feet and neck, tie her white shroud and ask

*Would you rather go to the State Prison, Rose?*


Just curious. *She stood like a lamb,* still, *dumb.*

She thought of the cart. *No. I had rather be hung.*

## April 25, 1822 : Samuel Green
*Boston, Massachusetts*

*My dear Mother,*

       *I now sit down to write*

*to you the last lines, attempt to inform*

*you, for the first time, of my fate. I was tried*

*for murder. Prisoners, to gain their liberty, swore*

*against me; and now I am condemned to die,*

*most likely before you receive this. I am afraid*

*this will likely break your heart. Dear mother, I might*

*have lived, might have been happy if I had staid*

*at home and taken your advice. Now I*

*am bound in irons and chained to the door—I shall*

*soon sink under my misfortunes. Give my*

*love to my sisters and cousins, those who called*

*themselves my friends. Bid them farewell, and then*

*try to forget you ever had a son.*

## April 22, 1831: Charles Gibbs
*Ellis Island, New York*

The court's death sentence for his piracy

and murders said it should be public, by hanging,

but then went further: his body, they decreed,

would go *to the College* to be dissected. Waiting

to die, he was heartened to hear of an attempt

to make hanging more humane, *painless*, quick

*by slinging them up, instead of dropping them.*

*Five fifty-six pound weights, rope* one inch thick,

two *pulleys, scaffold thirteen feet from the earth.*

Gibbs called the doctor, asked *in a lowered tone*

*could he die easier by holding his breath*

*or breathing out?* Perhaps *the latter mode.*

Rope cut, he was *drawn up* but struggled, freed

his hands and tore at the hood, dying to breathe.

# November 11, 1831: Nat Turner
*Jerusalem, Virginia*

Of course Turner's mind—*restless, inquisitive,*

*observant of every thing*—would turn his rage

to visions of *the Spirit* at work. He gives

accounts in his *Confession* of *spirits engaged*

*in battle, blood on the corn,* and hieroglyphs

on leaves that told him what to do. My class

in the prison disagrees, has trouble with

Nat Turner, with the visions, violent acts

against children who "never hurt him." Upset,

one blurts out, "I was tortured and abused

by my boyfriend, then killed some other guy, and that

ain't right. He's cold in the ground. What did he do

to me?" Next we review what they did when he died:

*flesh* rendered to *grease, a money-purse made of his hide.*

## January 31, 1850 : Reuben Dunbar
*Westerlo, New York*


Bad servant. Caliban alone with two

Mirandas. Savage and deformed, he lit

the fire, fetched the water, wood. He used

the swingle first to thresh corn, and then to hit

the younger's head. The ten year old he hanged.

Phrenologists examined him for days.

Sublimity, five. Form, six. Like Chang and Eng,

*his animal propensities outweigh*

*his moral faculties.* Combativeness,

six. Order, six. *He lacks true dignity*

*of character*, honor. Large destructiveness

and firmness. *Selfish, mean*, in God he sees

an *all-consuming fire*, a God of vengeance —

not one of mercy, kindness, benevolence.

## August 30, 1850: Professor John W. Webster
*Boston, Massachusetts*

When Charles Dickens came to Boston ten

years later, he asked to visit not the State

House, new or old; not the libraries, fens,

but the little basement with a furnace, great

in the public imagination. Gore. Hacked limbs

in black and white. The janitor, who heard

Parkman lend Webster money, found legs and ribs

in river water, waiting to be burned.


Webster's last night, he read Corinthians

with his wife and daughters: *O death, where is thy sting?*

*The sting of death is sin, and the strength of sin*

*is the law.* The crowd in the street saw everything.

The sheriff cried *God save the commonwealth*:

a hush, a clang, and Parkman's killer fell.

# December 2, 1859: John Brown
*Charlestown, Virginia*

*. . . awaiting the hour of my public murder with great*

*composure of mind and cheerfulness,* he wrote

his wife. Same hat, red slippers he'd worn to wait

the forty days and nights in jail. He rode

in a cart, oak coffin for a bench, and found

it *beautiful country.* He asked *be quick.* Tied

up, hooded on the platform, the rope around

his neck, he waited and waited as soldiers lined

up, performed their drills so long some whispered

*Shame! Shame!* At last the hatchet hit the rope,

a rope too short to kill him quick. He quivered,

jerked his limbs, reached for his neck, and choked.

His gallows: *glorious like the cross.* And in

two days another was built for the two black men.

## December 26, 1862: Chaska

*Mankato, Minnesota*

After the *massacre*, three hundred Sioux were tried

and condemned, but Lincoln made that thirty-eight.

They'd raped or murdered—one, Chaskadon, knifed

a pregnant woman, carved the baby out—

but Chaska got jail time; a woman testified

he'd saved her life.

                The gallows was a crowded

square built to hang, at once, *ten men each side.*

Singing in *doleful harmony*, hooded, bound,

*they tried to take one another by the hand.*

Sarah Wakefield, the woman Chaska saved,

read this in the papers, and saw that he'd been hanged.

Officials apologized for their mistake:

Chaskadon, not Chaska, was to have died.


*I am not ashamed to acknowledge that I cried.*

## June 19, 1863: Private William Grover
*Leesburgh, Virginia*

Walt Whitman was working in the hospital where

Grover's brother ended up, wounded in battle:

—*poor unfortunate boy—good looking dark haired*

*fellow*—fevered, grieving a brother who hadn't

had a furlough in two years. Was brave, but missed

his mother. Whitman listened to him, imagined

*the countless officers' straps, the gaud and tinsel,*

*this show of general stars & bars, this pageant*

and *that single simple boy, who had stood*

not *flinching, not yet nineteen years of age,*

*the volley—the smoke—the body and the blood.*


> *Young man I think I know you—I think this face*
> *is the face of the Christ himself, Dead and divine*
> *and brother of all, and here again he lies.*

## April 22, 1864: Corporal William B. Jones
*Kinston, North Carolina*

They left the South and got caught with the North, so Jones

and twenty-one others were court martialed for desertion

and kept for weeks in a *dungeon* not far from his home.

His wife brought food. Some got baptismal *immersion*

in the Neuse. The preacher called them *vicious*, diseased

and wicked, hoped they were *prepared for their doom.*

Two one day, five the next, the third fifteen

hanged *from one pole.* When she tried to bring him home,

*the rebels cursed her:* some bodies were sold to surgeons

*like common felons,* or *scooped in a common grave*

*at the foot of the gallows.* After a week their son,

fifteen, went back for the body. *The doctor gave*

*him it, which was stripped of all covering excepting the socks.*

Saved from dissection, buried on a borrowed lot.

## July 7, 1865: Mary Eugenia Surratt
*Old Arsenal Prison, District of Columbia*

The executioner's name was Christian Rath;

the prison, soldiers, gallows unbearably hot.

*Not enough evidence to hang a cat,*

but Lincoln was dead, the actor tracked and shot,

so the landlady, *traitress*, walked *between two priests*;

hands, ankles in irons, a bonnet on her head.

She was *dressed and veiled in black*, her face unseen.

Rath clapped: the *two drops fell with a sickening thud.*

*I lifted her, not being willing that any*

*hand should desecrate her.* Untied her gown,

arms, *removed the noose, her limp body bending,*

*placed her in the box with my own hands, alone.*


When I untied her, taking her body down,

some *heartless* man said *she makes a good bow.*

# November 10, 1865: Major Henry Wirz
*Old Arsenal Prison, District of Columbia*

The pictures of Andersonville prison: makeshift tents,

latrines. Emaciated men. Mass graves

lined with naked corpses, stripped by their friends

and *stacked like cordwood*. Mud. The water made

the tiniest cut a death sentence: *gangrene,*

*scurvy, maggots, diarrhea, lice.*

WIRZ BOASTS OF KILLING MORE YANKEES THAN GEN. LEE:

some months *nearly every other man died.*

He was tried for war crimes, argued he *simply obeyed*

*the legal orders of his superiors.*

He was calm on the scaffold in his black shroud, prayed,

but had no last words. His former prisoners

climbed trees to see, so they could say they were there

*and the Andersonville jailor was dangling in the air.*

## December 12, 1884: George Cooke
*Laramie, Wyoming*

He drank all night and then all day, and fought

his brother-in-law in the street. He killed him. The one

who saw the murder said after he fired the shot

and James Blunt fell, Cooke looked a little stunned

and walked around to address the torn, burnt head:

*Son of a bitch: I've killed you, have I?* His defense

was simple: *not responsible*, they said,

*by reason of being crazy drunk.* No chance.


On the scaffold, his gait and voice were *firm and clear:*

*It was at once evident to all that Cook*

*meant to die game.* Reporters saw not fear,

but *wonderful courage.* The next day, readers could look

at the front page of the LARAMIE BOOMERANG

to see Cooke face this headline: HE DIED GAME.

## August 6, 1890 : William Kemmler
*Auburn, New York*

In Euripides' *Medea*, Medea kills

her rival with a poisoned robe and crown.

She doesn't get to watch. The play is filled

with hearsay and reporting: Princess, *unsound*

*in every limb. White froth* on her lips. The screams,

*unnatural devouring fire.* The messenger,

unnamed, describes how *dripped blood mixed with flames*;

he takes his time, *doubles* Medea's pleasure.


The first electrocution New York botched

was Kemmler's. *Electric execution*: new,

humane. A man strapped down. Reporters watched

his new suit burn, called in *singed hair, shined shoes.*

*Blood stood* in his pores. *Smoke* rose above his head.

*The smell of burning flesh*, and he was dead.

# June 28, 1895: Michael McDonough
*Columbus, Ohio*

Say he's my great great grandfather. Or say

he's yours. CLEVELAND PRESS — *FRESH OHIO NEWS* —

put our grandfather's hanging on the sports page,

after THE DEADLY CIGARET and *soon*

*C. Grimes will start in business, giving baths.*

McDonough's headline's hard to find, and then

it's SICKENING. *Awful Scene at the Gallows. As*

*Shocking* and *Gory as a Guillotine.*

He'd *stabbed his wife to death on a dark bridge*, lost

his case and spent a year in prison where

he *had grown heavy, his flesh and muscles soft.*

His head came off. *Blood spurted* in the air,

*upon the spectators, executioners.*

And on *the prison physicians, bloody as butchers.*

## October 29, 1901: Leon Czolgosz
*Auburn, New York*

A thousand people saw him at the front

of the hall, lined up to shake McKinley's hand.

Some helped the secret service hold him, punch

his stomach so he couldn't fire again.

The jury needed less than half an hour.

He said he wasn't sorry: *He was shouting*

*prosperity when there was none for the poor.*

*I've done my duty. I don't believe in voting.*

He got the chair, and went to prison to wait.

Crowds gathered when they brought him, mauled him so

he bled, frothed at the mouth, passed out. The state

gave him one thousand seven hundred volts

two times. He lurched, gave off some steam. And when

they felt no pulse, they flipped the switch again.

# June 9, 1916 : Juan Sanchez
*Deming, New Mexico*

*Natives* cut hemp, tore and hackled it by hand,

baled fiber, shipped it to Tubbs Cordage factory

where men still shake out tangles, dirt and sand,

and feed hemp to successive combing machines

until it pours *as water from a hose.*

Slivers spin clockwise into yarn, then double

back in strands, reverse again to rope,

so *all good rope is absolutely neutral.*


San Quentin's warden sent the sheriff heights,

weights, two good ropes, a schedule. Grease the line

with *mutton tallow*; put *the knot behind*

*his left ear.* After Sanchez was hanged, cut down,

he came to life on the ground : breathing, but not

conscious. They carried him back up to the drop.

## February 8, 1924: Gee Jon
*Carson City, Nevada*

In San Francisco, assault and murder among

the hatchet men of Chinatown were said

to be *as plentiful as blackberries.* The tongs

controlled gambling, *daughters of joy, hopheads*

from there to here. The D. A. argued the Chinese

can't tell right from wrong. *Inferior.*

Hanging had been Nevada's standard means

of execution; gas would be modern, more

humane. They practiced first on bedbugs. The day

before, the CHUNG SAI YAT PO reported some

kittens successfully gassed, and *a large white stray.*

At twenty to ten, they led him, weeping, from

his cell to the chamber. In minutes he *ceased to move.*

Ten-twenty: fans on. Doors unsealed at noon.

## August 23, 1927: Nicola Sacco
*Charlestown, Massachusetts*

Vanzetti said to quit the hunger strike,

but Sacco stalled: why fatten up before

you're killed? When he ate, he ate for strength to write

*Be strong, dear Dante. Comfort your mother.* Or

*Ines, in every angle, this sad walled cell*

*and everywhere my gaze rests, I love you*

*much, then so much.* On the twenty-third, the tall

doors of the Athenaeum's Reading Room

saw someone slip small fliers into all

the magazines: *their voices are gone, but will*

*be remembered in gratitude and tears.* Exalted

shall be these *working men and dreamers,* killed

by *Judges, Scholars, Governors* whose names

*have gone down into everlasting shame.*

# August 23, 1927: Bartolomeo Vanzetti
*Charlestown, Massachusetts*

He finally saw the *nighty, starry sky*
with guards escorting him from cell to death
house. Seven years, a judge who'd ask with pride
*Did you see what I did to those anarchist bastards?* Yet
he knew, without them, he would have lived and died
*unmarked, unknown, a failure.* With *some sins,*
*but never crime. I've never committed crime*
*at all, at all.*

When Socrates' jailer came in
with the hemlock, he wept for Socrates, *the finest,*
*best-tempered man of any in that place.*

Vanzetti thanked his jailers for their kindness,
their help. They tightened straps and covered his face.
His warden wept when Vanzetti murmured he
would forgive *some people for what they are doing to me.*

## August 14, 1936: Rainey Bethea
*Owensboro, Kentucky*

He raped a grandmother to death. She bled

to death, bled on *his privates*, died before

he took her rings and left her dirtied bed.

He left his ring behind, initialled 'R'.


The other blacks in town offered to burn

him themselves.

          Just murder and he'd get the chair,

but black men who raped white women still earned

a public hanging.


          In photographs, his hair's

neat, waved. Head tilted, insolent and just

baptized, pale collar open at the neck.

The hot dogs, drunken hangman, white crowd that rushed

to snatch his hood—that hasn't happened yet.


Thousands wrote the sheriff: "It was wrong."

Or "*Hang more niggers. We're with you thousands strong.*"

## January 31, 1945: Private Eddie D. Slovik
*Saint Marie, France*

Twelve riflemen with loaded rifles, lined

across from Private Slovik. One of the guns

is loaded with blanks, but they all take aim to find

him in their sights, blindfolded, shocked in the sun.

The priest has pinned a target to his chest.


*Deserter. Coward.* He'd written his C. O.

that he was left behind in France, confessed

I'LL RUN AWAY AGAIN IF I HAVE TO GO

OUT THEIR. The men he deserted thought he'd get

let off with prison time, dishonor. When

the twelve heard they'd been picked they never thought

they'd really kill him; they hadn't killed their own

since '64, but in '45 they'd start:

a firing squad, too stunned to hit his heart.

## May 3, 1946: Willie Francis

*Saint Martinsville, Louisiana*

They brought Louisiana's only chair

in a pick-up from Angola into Saint

Martinsville Parish, to the Court House, where

a fifteen-year-old colored boy had lain

on straw for months. Jailhouse on the second floor:

Death kindly took the elevator. Wires

were tossed from dynamo to window. Four

men setting up the chair passed flasks, dead tired

and innocent of amps. They called the priest,

and pulled the switch, and thought he'd die. He shook

and lurched and gasped — *You're not supposed to breathe!*

They shut it down, freed him from straps and hood.

Then Willie Francis stood up without help

and — miracle, miracle — walked back to his cell.

## May 9, 1947: Willie Francis
*Saint Martinsville, Louisiana*

The TIMES reporters asked him to describe
the taste of death. *Cold peanut butter.* Fair
stars, little speckles: *pink and green, like shines*
*in a rooster's tail.* He said *God fool'd with the chair.*

His father smashed his gravestone into slivers
of granite. Hundreds wrote *divine intervention,*
how *gold electrodes would corrode* and silver
wires short if they tried to kill that boy again.
Like Daniel in the lion's den; those men
in Nebuchadnezzar's furnace; unusual; cruel;
double jeopardy: none of that could save him.
At noon the chair was ready, voltage full.
He said *everything is all right* and died
without pink stars, green, anything divine.

## June 19, 1953: Julius and Ethel Rosenberg
*Ossining, New York*

Electrocution set for eight p.m.

Two hours before they took him to be prepped

the matrons asked her if she'd like to see him;

the warden said that they could take some steps

to let them talk. A screen of metal mesh

between two wooden chairs outside her cell.

Romantic. Pyramus and Thisbe, rushed

in writing letters to their kids, to tell

them *Remember: we were innocent, and could*

*not wrong our conscience. Now we press you close*

*and kiss you with all our strength.* Before they stood

to go he kissed two fingers, pressed them both

against the screen, to hers: first white, then red.

Their final touch, through screen. So hard they bled.

## May 2, 1960: Caryl Chessman
*San Quentin, California*

No one had ever shown the inside out:

the *chains, cold water, grayness of dawn*. He wrote

bestselling memoirs, described *the doomed* around

him, kept his name in papers and in court.

Twelve years of *slippers, cafeteria trays,*

appeal briefs, petitions for writs of mandate,

rehearing, *habeas corpus*. Petitions for stays.

Not a bad lawyer: he avoided dying eight

of his nine scheduled deaths. Brando, Brigitte Bardot

wrote Eisenhower, said Chessman did not belong

in *this stupid, obscene place called Death Row*.

After his ninth appeal, he walked along

*dark green walls* to a *steel room*, an odor he'd

described in print as *peach blossoms, sickening-sweet*.

## April 14, 1965: Perry Smith
*Lansing, Kansas*

Truman Capote's *In Cold Blood* recounts

the recurring dream that Smith kept having on Death

Row: *A Vegas night club. He's dancing around,*

singing. A stage with *gold-painted prop-steps.*

At the top he bows to *no applause, none,* though

the place is packed, with *Negroes, mostly. Men.*

He understands, at once, that they are *ghosts,*

*ghosts of the hanged, and he's there to join them:*

*the gold-painted steps have led to a scaffold.*

The trap door opens beneath him, *his top hat tumbles,*

and he falls. *Urinates, defecates,* dies—starts, baffled,

awake.


The *warehouse* was *dingy, cluttered with lumber:*

*thirteen steps, noose, black mask.* No hymn, no psalm.

He spat out his gum in *the chaplain's outstretched palm.*

# January 17, 1977 : Gary Gilmore
*Point of the Mountain, Utah*

A life of crime, of theft and drugs and jail

in Oregon and Illinois, but when

he robbed a Provo gas station, motel,

he shot and killed two clerks, both Mormon men —

Max Jensen and Ben Bushnell — with wives and sons.

*There are sins that the blood of a calf, of a lamb*

*or doves cannot remit. They must be atoned*

*by the blood of man.*


He asked to *die like a man,*

and did, chained to *a regular green chair.*

When asked for last words, he said *Let's do it.*

*Black T-shirt, white pants.* They added a hood, their

target, *then bang, bang, bang, three noises, quick.*


A line from Gilmore's mother that I found :

*They shot your brother's heart out, on the ground.*

# December 7, 1982: Charles Brooks
*Huntsville, Texas*

Before the first lethal injection, doctors decided

it violates the Hippocratic Oath,

so *technicians* got the job. Physicians confided

that *it can take hours and be a real bloodbath.*

*It's not like a tetanus shot*; if you miss the vein,

it's *excruciating.* Witnesses watched as Brooks,

*in gold pants, brown shirt open to the waist,*

*lay on a gurney, restrained by six straps.* He took

*a long deep yawn. Two needles in his arm,*

*blood splatters on the sheet.* He *wheezed, gasped*: death

*did not appear to be painless.*


*First, do no harm*

the papers would read the next day. In Brooks' last breaths

he prayed *I bear witness there is no God*

*but Allah. Unto Allah do we belong.*

# April 16, 1986: Daniel Morris Thomas
*Starke, Florida*

SCREAMING KILLER IS EXECUTED    6

MEN NEEDED TO STRAP THOMAS INTO CHAIR: *Get*

*off me or I'll kill you!* He fought, swore, *kicked*

a guard *in the groin, tried to bite* one, and hit

two others. He *struggled seven minutes.*


                                        *The son*

*of poor Mississippi blacks who claimed he had*

*been "terrorized" by the Ku Klux Klan when young,*

he shot a professor and raped his wife as the man

*lay dying.* Then he *shot the family dog.*


Restrained, resigned, he read out his final words:

*We are human tools and political pawns*

*for human sacrifice,* he said, breathing hard.

His *black hooded executioner* was *paid*

*$150 by the state.*

## May 21, 1997:  Bruce Edwin Callins
*Huntsville, Texas*


The nation's highest court heard arguments on

the constitutionality of Texas' death

penalty. They decided it was fine,

except for Justice Blackmun. In his dissent—

*From this day forward, I no longer shall*

*tinker with the machinery of death*—he wrote

*that the death penalty experiment has failed.*


It was Callins' case, and he wrote a thank you note

to Blackmun, for shedding light *on what it means*

*to be poor, and not have a proper education,*

*particularly in Texas.* His death was routine:

the staff at Huntsville was used to lethal injections,

and under the new governor there were more

than usual. This was the governor's thirty-fourth.

## June 22, 2000 : Gary Graham, later known as Shaka Sankofa
*Huntsville, Texas*

When Bobby Lambert was shot outside the Stop

& Shop, five witnesses saw the shooter run

away. One said it was Graham. Four others thought

the shooter was *darker, smaller*. Doubt, wrong gun,

no fingerprints, but his lawyer, Ronald Mock,

was a joke ; Graham joined *The Mock Wing* on death row

at seventeen. In his final words, he talked

about *what is happening tonight in America*. Crowds

gathered. Some chanted *George Bush, you can't hide!*

*We charge you with genocide!* A sign

held by one Ku Klux Klansman : awkward lines

of hand-drawn syringes, a scrawled DIE N-WORD !DIE!

*The injection took effect* at 8:49.


*This is a lynching. They are murdering me tonight.*

## August 9, 2000: Brian Roberson
*Huntsville, Texas*

On a night of *drinking, smoking PCP*

*mixed with formaldehyde*, he stabbed his neighbors,

a white couple, and killed them. He said he believed

he did it, but couldn't imagine why, since *they were*

*the nicest people on the block.*

His father

was stabbed to death by a white junkie when Brian

was ten: not a mitigating factor

but a motive, according to the court. So *why*

*is it that white man who murdered my husband got*

*thirteen years?* Brian's mother asked.

His last

words were for *racist white folks, black folks who hate*

*themselves, the words of my famous brother Nat*

*Turner: y'all kiss my black ass.* Smiling, he died,

and they cleared the room for the next injection that night.

## August 9, 2000: Oliver Cruz
*Huntsville, Texas*

He *raped* Kelly Donovan, *stabbed her 20 times*

and *left her body alongside the road.* The state

said *he may not be very smart*, but tried

this out: *it makes him more dangerous.* He made

some progress, his years in prison: *I can write*

*a letter, a half a page.* He didn't know

what *retarded* meant. When he went to the chamber to die,

*sobbing, teary-eyed,* he said *Take me home,*

*Jesus. I'm sorry.* When there's only one

lethal injection a night, it's at six, but Cruz

went half an hour after Roberson.

*The same chamber, same gurney,* but they used

*new sheets, needles, and tubing* for each one.

Five minutes after strapping in Cruz they were done.

# June 11, 2001: Timothy McVeigh
*Terre Haute, Indiana*

Victims' loved ones in Oklahoma City

gathered to watch on closed circuit TV;

*security* kept *hackers from stealing the signal.*

His lawyer said McVeigh *was able to see*

*the moon in the sky* on the way to the death house, and that

meant something to him. Viewers saw his *face*

*hard as stone, face of evil. His eyes looked black.*

He stared at the camera, jaw clenched, *the face of hate.*

His eyes *rolled back when his heart stopped* and he died.

Most saw *The Devil,* back *in hell,* which caused

one man to say *He's not a monster, guys,*

*not when you're looking him in the face.* He paused.

*There's no facial expressions on him, so there's*

*no way of knowing exactly what he is.*

## October 9, 2002: Aileen Wuornos
*Starke, Florida*

That makeup on Charlize Theron, and how

the murders piled up; the first in self-

defense, then all the rest. In theatres, crowds

of people streamed out: silent, shocked. Her death

warrant's online: Adobe Acrobat.

And Netflix has two documentaries

with interviews and trials, old photographs.

She says she's getting *all the tears out of me*

*and stuff so I won't cry and jazz. To tough*

*it out as tough as I can.* This used to be

called "dying game." In the end, that wasn't enough:

*You sabotaged my ass, society!*

*Inhumane fucking living bastards and bitches*

*who used me for money, for books, and movies and shit.*

## September 3, 2003: Paul Hill
*Starke, Florida*

In the paper the women were weeping. Pixelled tear

stained women, stunned outside the prison in Starke.


Hill bought a shotgun, practiced shooting near

the Pensacola Ladies Center, parked

and waited, shot and killed, reloaded, killed

again. He put the gun down, met the cops,

his face down on the asphalt, very still.


The women in the paper wept when the shot

of sodium pentothal stopped his beating heart.

They held each other up, or knelt to pray.

They cried that Florida made Paul Hill a martyr

and the Bible justifies his work, his way

to rescue babies: *Whosoever sheds*

*the blood of man, by man shall his blood be shed.*

## May 13, 2005 : Michael Ross
*Somers, Connecticut*

*I am one of the greatest of sinners. I have murdered*
*eight women in a horrible way.* The papers
lined up eight photos, smiling girls with feathered
hair posing at school or parties. Wendy, April,
Dzung, Paula, Debra, Robin, Leslie, and Tammy
*were dead as soon as I saw them,* he confessed.


A *volunteer,* he wanted to spare their families.
Or die, or get attention. Or he had *Death*
*Row Syndrome,* was a *malignant narcissist.*
Outside the prison, supporters told reporters
*What do we do with trash? We bury it.*
Inside, *strapped to a table,* Ross *gasped and shuddered*
while Robin's sister watched. She said *It was too*
*peaceful. But I'm sure I will feel some closure soon.*

# Notes

Watt Espy's database of executions from 1608 to 1987 was very helpful; it's available online at www.deathpenaltyinfo.org. Searchable by date, state, and name, it provided both a quick reference and a constant reminder of the scale of the task. Stuart Banner's book, *The Death Penalty: An American History* was published two years after I started my project, right around the time I was starting to get overwhelmed by the absence of a book like his. It is at once thorough, concise, and well-written; the bibliography has been very useful in tracking down primary sources for these executions.

Banner also provides a more recent look into Espy's work than is available online: "The closest estimate we have comes from the work of Watt Espy, who as of December 1998 had compiled information on 19,248 executions in the United States and its colonial predecessors, in the form of paper files in his house in Alabama." If Espy's figures are correct, there were 19,752 legal executions here between 1608 and 2005.

The following notes provide bibliographic information for useful sources; texts listed in the "Quotations" section are quoted, in italics, in the poems.

### Early 1608: George Kendall
The first documented execution in American history. The Jamestown colony was founded in May, 1606; Kendall was one of the seven men in the colony's council. Within a year, he and another member were exiled, charged with theft and other crimes. John Smith kept the best record of this period, although he does not provide an exact date for the execution.

Mapp, Alf J. *The Virginia Experiment: The Old Dominion's Role in the Making of America, 1607–1781.* Lanham, MD: Hamilton Press, 1987

Watson, Aldren A. *The Village Blacksmith.* New York: Crowell, 1968

QUOTATIONS: Ashton, John, ed. *The Adventures and Discourses of Captain John Smith, sometime president of Virginia, and Admiral of New England.* London: Cassell, 1883

Smith, John. "A True Relation of Such Occurences and accidents of noate as have happened in Virginia since the first planting of the collony, which is now resident in the South part thereof, till the last returne from thence." *Southern Literary Messenger*, v. 11, 1845

### 1659, 1660: Mary Dyer
Dyer's two death sentences were the result of her religious beliefs; spreading Quakerism was a capital crime in colonial Boston. There's a statue of Dyer at the state house in Boston, across from the Boston Athenaeum; the

Granary Burying Ground is on the other side of the Athenaeum. Some accounts indicate she's buried there; others suggest she was buried near the Old Elm, where she was hanged on the Common. Hodges' sketch describes Dyer's conscious choice to return to Boston: "Thus she had her will and offered herself,—our New England Iphigeneia,—a sacrifice for the common good."

Hodges, George. *The Apprenticeship of Washington and Other Sketches of Significant Colonial Personages.* New York: Moffat, Yard and Co. 1909

McClellan, Elisabeth. *History of American Costume, 1607–1870.* New York: Tudor Publishing Company, 1937

QUOTATIONS: Barber, Samuel. *Boston Common; a diary of notable events, incidents, and neighboring occurences.* Boston: Christopher Publishing House, 1914

Rogers, Horatio. *Mary Dyer of Rhode Island: The Quaker Martyr that was hanged on Boston Common June 1, 1660.* Providence: Preston and Rounds, 1896

### 1692: Susanna Martin

Martin was rebuked for laughing at the behavior of her supposedly possessed accusers, and replied, "Well I may at such folly."

Karlsen, Carol F. *The Devil in the Shape of a Woman: Witchcraft in Colonial New England.* New York: Vintage Books, 1987

QUOTATIONS: Mather, Cotton. *Wonders of the Invisible World.* London: J. R. Smith, 1862

### 1715: Margaret Gaulacher

Not much is known about Gaulacher; Watt Espy records her name as Callahan. She refused to thank Cotton Mather for his spiritual guidance, and died without repenting.

QUOTATIONS: *The Boston Newsletter*

Mather, Cotton. *A sorrowful spectacle: in two sermons, occasined by a just sentence of death, on a miserable woman, for the murder of a spurious offspring.* Boston: T. Fleet & T. Crump, 1715

### 1726: William Fly

After leading the mutiny that made him a pirate, he renamed the ship "Fame's Revenge." He carried flowers to his execution, and was gibbeted at Nix's Mate island in Boston Harbor, a popular place for the display of executed pirates.

QUOTATIONS: Mather, Cotton. *The vial poured out upon the sea: A remarkable relation of certain pirates brought unto a tragical and untimely end.* Boston: T. Fleet, 1726

Colman, Benjamin. *It is a fearful thing to fall into the hands of the living God: A Sermon preached to some miserable pirates July 10, 1726.* Boston: John Phillips and Thomas Hancock, 1726

### 1755: Tom, A Negro

There are several instances in colonial Virginia of slaves executed for petit treason and quartered for display. While Tom's trial is relatively well-documented, and John Clark's testimony recorded, there is no record of anything Tom said beyond his plea.

[54]

Keve, Paul W. *The History of Corrections in Virginia*. Charlottesville: University Press of Virginia, 1986

QUOTATIONS: *Amelia County Order Book*, 1751–1735, "Trial of Tom," Feb 25, 1755

DeLorme Mapping Company. *Virginia Atlas and Gazetteer*. Yarmouth, DeLorme Mapping, 2000

## 1755: Mark and Phillis

After a failed attempt to burn down their master's house in the hopes that he'd be forced to sell them to someone kinder, Mark, Phillis, and another slave began poisoning him. When Paul Revere wrote about his famous ride, he used "where Mark was hanged in chains" as a landmark.

Revere, Paul. *Paul Revere's three accounts of his famous ride*. Boston: Massachusetts Historical Society, 1961

QUOTATIONS: Goodell, Abner Cheney. *The trial and execution, for petit treason, of Mark and Phillis: slaves of Capt. John Codman, who murdered their master at Charlestown, Mass., in 1755; for which the man was hanged and gibbeted, and the woman was burned to death; including, also, some account of other punishments by burning in Massachusetts.* Cambridge: J. Wilson and Son, 1883

## 1773: Levi Ames

Ames' execution was very well-attended and publicized; Andrew Eliot, Samuel Mather, and Samuel Stillman all published sermons based on his trial, imprisonment, and execution. Mather's contains Ames' dying confession, and Stillman's includes the conversation on "the souls of the wicked."

QUOTATIONS: Mather, Samuel. *Christ sent to heal the broken hearted. A sermon, preached at the Thursday lecture in Boston, on October, 21st. 1773. when Levi Ames, a young man, under sentence of death for burglary, to be executed on that day, was present to hear the discourse.* Boston: William M'Alpine, 1773

Stillman, Samuel. *Two sermons: the first from Psalm CII. 19, 20. Delivered the Lords-Day before the execution of Levi Ames, who was executed at Boston, Thursday October 21. 1773. for burglary. Aet. 22. This discourse was preached at the desire of the criminal, who also attended on the occasion. The second from Proverbs XVII. 25. Preached the Lords-Day after his execution; and designed as an improvement of that awful event, by way of caution to others. To which is added, at the request of many, an account of the exercise of his mind, from the time of his condemnation, till he left the world; together with the conversation the author had with him as he walked with him from the prison to the gallows. By all which, compared with his latter conduct, he may be thought in a judgment of charity, to have died, a penitent thief.* Boston: J. Kneeland for P. Freeman, 1773

## 1778: Aaaran

Part of the problem between the Spanish and the Pamo was that the Pamo women were interested in the Spanish soldiers. When missionaries attempted to intervene, the women pointed out that their men were busy fishing all the time, and "los soldades son guapos": the soldiers are handsome. "Come and be slain" is Bancroft's translation of Aaaran's message. The last line refers to the fact that Aaaran and the others would of course be executed whether or not the priest was able to save their souls.

QUOTATIONS: Bancroft, Hubert Howe. *History of California*. San Francisco: The History Company, 1890
*State Papers Sacramento Series v. 1, Provincial Records 1, 8*

### 1789: Rachel Wall

Wall was a maid on Beacon Hill until she became a pirate with her husband George; when he left her, she took up residence in a "bawdy-house" and supplemented her income with theft. Although she mentions many crimes in her confession, her execution is for a count of highway robbery Wall denied. She was accused of knocking down Margaret Bender on the street, shoving a handkerchief in her mouth, and taking her shoes and bonnet.

QUOTATIONS: Wall, Rachel. *Life, Last Words, and Dying Confession of Rachel Wall*. Boston: 1789

### 1797: Abraham Johnstone

Johnstone was hanged "for the murder of Thomas Read, a Guinea negro." The introduction of his "Address" reassures the reader of its authenticity: "the account of his life is strongly corroborated by a Mulatto man and his wife, both of respectable characters." His speech provides a critical history of slavery in America from 1606 to the time of his death.

QUOTATIONS: Johnstone, Abraham. *The Address of Abraham Johnstone, a Black Man, Who Was Hanged at Woodbury, in the County of Glocester, and State of New Jersey, on Saturday the 8th Day of July Last; to the People of Colour. To Which Is Added His Dying Confession or Declaration. Also, a Copy of a Letter to His Wife, Written the Day Previous to His Execution*. Philadelphia: The Purchasers, 1797 Available online at www.docsouth.ch.edu, the website of Documenting the American South, a terrific resource for hard-to-find texts.

### 1819: Rose Butler

Butler, a slave, was convicted of burning down her mistress' house; she was the last person publicly hanged and buried on the potter's field that became Washington Square. The account of her execution includes a conversation she had with her jailors, in which she said she'd rather be hanged than go to the state prison. Shortly after her execution a separate prison was built in New York for women prisoners, but in 1819 women were still incarcerated in the attic of the men's prison at Auburn.

Janvier, Thomas. *In Old New York*. New York: St. Martin's Press, 2000

Powers, Gershom. *A brief account of the construction, management, and discipline &c. &c. the New York State Prison at Auburn: together with a comendium on criminal law. Also a report of the trial of an officer of said prison for whipping a convict.* Auburn: U.F. Doubleday, 1826

QUOTATIONS: Ripley, Dorothy. *An account of Rose Butler, aged nineteen years, whose execution I attended in the potter's field*. New York: John C. Totten, 1819

### 1822: Samuel Green

In his confession, Green lists all the things he can remember stealing, including penknives, silk, a bottle of brandy, some crackers and cheese, a mare, watch chains, elegant diamond breast pins, and a screw auger. He escaped from most of the prisons in New England with the help of his friend "A.":

"It may seem surprising to those who read this sketch of my life, how it was possible that when I was in difficulty, he by some means or other, found out where I was; but I am sure if he had been a thousand miles from me, and heard I was in prison, he would have lost no time in coming to see me at the risk of his life. I believe there were never two people closer linked together by ties of friendship than we were, for as long as we were acquainted and in as many different scenes we have acted, whether good or bad, we never had one word of dispute of any kind, whatever he had was mine, and mine was his, and we always divided our money equally to one cent." Green was in the Boston jail when a group of inmates planned escape; Billy Williams, a black convict, informed on the white conspirators. He was murdered shortly afterward; Green was convicted of the crime and hanged for it. The end of his confession is a letter to his mother, Mercy Q. Green, who hadn't heard from him since he ran away as a young man: "I was sent to prison the 3d of July, 1818, and have been in prison ever since. I am now in Boston gaol and shall be executed within thirty days."

QUOTATIONS: Green, Samuel. *Life of Samuel Green, executed at Boston, April 25, 1822, for the murder of Billy Williams, a fellow convict with Green, in the state prison.* Boston: D. Felt, 1822

## 1831: Charles Gibbs
Gibbs, a pirate, confessed to four hundred murders, explaining "It is murder as much to stand by and encourage the deed, as to stab with a knife, strike with a hatchet, or shoot with a pistol." His final words: "I hope that Christ will make my death as easy as if I had died on a downy pillow."

Banner, Stuart. *The Death Penalty: An American History.* Cambridge: Harvard University Press, 2002

Gibbs, Charles. *Mutiny and murder. Confession of Charles Gibbs, a native of Rhode Island, who, with Thomas J. Wansley, was doomed to be hung in New York on the 22nd of April last, for the murder of the captain and mate of the brig Vinyard . . . Annexed is a solemn address to youth.* Providence: Israel Smith, 1831

QUOTATIONS: *Morning Courier and New-York Enquirer*

## 1831: Nat Turner
Turner led a rebellion in which more than forty slaves killed about fifty-five slave owners. In the aftermath of the rebellion, fifty-five people were legally executed, and more than two hundred were murdered by white mobs.

QUOTATIONS: Turner, Nat. *The Confessions of Nat Turner, The Leader of the Late Insurrection in Southampton, Virginia.* Baltimore: Thomas R. Gray, 1831 Available online at www.docsouth.ch.edu.

Drewry, William Sidney. *The Southampton Insurrection.* Washington: The Neal Company, 1900

## 1850: Reuben Dunbar
Dunbar murdered two boys, eight and ten years old, who stood to inherit the farm that had belonged to his father. The ten year old was hanged on a hemlock tree. The last recorded words of Stephen, the eight year old, were "Uncle, you buy me a fish hook, and I will catch you a big fish."

*Trial of Reuben Dunbar for the Murder of Stephen V. Lester and David C. Lester, 8 and 10 years of age.* Albany: P. C. Gilbert, 1850

*American Phrenological Journal.* New York: Fowlers and Wells, 1851

QUOTATIONS: Thompson, Margaret. *Phrenological Character of Reuben Dunbar.* Albany: P. C. Gilbert, 1851

## 1850: John Webster

Webster, a professor at Harvard, borrowed money from a lot of people, including George Parkman, another professor. When he didn't return the money, Parkman called him a scoundrel and a liar, and said he'd get him fired. In his confession, Webster described what happened next: "I felt nothing but the sting of his words. I was excited to the highest degree of passion and while he was speaking and gesticulating in the most violent and menacing manner, thrusting the letter and his fist into my face, in my fury I seized whatever thing was handiest—it was a stick of wood—and dealt him an instantaneous blow with all the force that passion could give it. . . . There was no second blow." Parkman's disappearance, the janitor's discovery of Webster's guilt, the trial, and the execution were all covered in the papers in detail.

*Boston Courier*

*Boston Transcript*

Bremer, Frederika. *Homes of the New World; Impressions of America.* London: A. Hall, Virtue & Co., 1853

Thompson, Helen. *Murder at Harvard.* Boston: Houghton Mifflin, 1971

Webster, John. *Trial of Prof. John W. Webster, for the murder of Dr. George Parkman, Nov. 23, 1849.* Boston: Daily Mail, 1850

## 1859: John Brown

Brown led a raid of the federal arsenal at Harpers Ferry, Virginia; he planned to steal weapons and arm slaves for an uprising, but was caught and convicted of treason. It was Thoreau who referred to his gallows as "glorious like the cross."

Redpath, James. *The Public Life of Capt. John Brown.* Boston: Thayer and Eldridge, 1860

Sanborn, F. B. ed. *John Brown's Life and Letters.* Boston: Roberts Brothers, 1885

Taft, S. H. *Discourse on the character and death of John Brown, delivered in Martinsburgh, NY Dec 12, 1859.* Des Moines: Steam Printing House of Carter, Hussey, and Curl, 1859

QUOTATIONS: Patton, William Weston. *The Execution of John Brown.* Chicago: Church, Goodman & Cushing, 1859

Thoreau, Henry D. *A Plea for Captain John Brown. Read to the citizens of Concord on Sunday evening, October thirtieth, eighteen fifty-nine.* Boston: D. R. Godine, 1969

## 1862: Chaska

The hanging of thirty-eight Dakota indians was the largest mass execution in American history. Wakefield, a white woman, believed that Chaska was executed on purpose, as punishment for the close relationship he was perceived to have had with her. I used Flandrau's account of the construction of the gallows and Berghold's account of the execution. The last line is from Wakefield's account.

Chomsky, Carol. "The United States–Dakota War Trials: A Study in Military Injustice." *Stanford Law Review*, Nov. 1990

Heard, Isaac V. D. *History of the Sioux War and Massacres of 1862 and 1863*. New York: Harper and Brothers, 1864

QUOTATIONS: Berghold, Alexander. *The Indians' Revenge, or Days of Horror: Some Appalling Events in the History of the Sioux*. San Francisco: P. J. Thomas, 1891

Flandrau, Charles E. *Narrative of the Indian War of 1862–1864 And Following Campaigns in Minnesota*. St. Paul: Civil and Indian Wars Commission, 1898

Wakefield, Sarah. *Six Weeks in the Sioux Tepees: A Narrative of Indian Captivity*. June Namias, Ed. Norman: University of Oklahoma Press, 1997

### 1863: Private William Grover

Grover was executed for desertion from the Union Army. Whitman met Grover's brother and father shortly after the execution, and recorded his thoughts in the small notebook he carried when he visited the hospital. Glicksberg reprints this in part, and Gayle Richardson, assistant librarian at the Huntington, transcribed it for me in full. The last three lines are from Whitman's "A Sight in Camp."

Glicksberg, Charles, ed. *Walt Whitman and the Civil War*. Philadelphia: UP Press, 1933

Lowenfels, Walter, ed. *Walt Whitman's Civil War*. New York: Knopf, 1960

*New York Herald*

QUOTATIONS: Whitman, Walt. *Hospital Notebook* Entry for June 25, 1863. At the Huntington Library.

Whitman, Walt. *Leaves of Grass*. New York: Crowell, 1902

Whitman, Walt. "William Grover Shot for Desertion."
www.digitalgallery.nypl.org

### 1864: Corporal William B. Jones

Jones was one of fifty-three men of the Second North Carolina Union Volunteer Regiment captured by Confederate Generals George Pickett and Robert Hoke. Twenty-seven of the prisoners were found to be Confederate soldiers who had deserted. Twenty-two were publicly hanged in Kinston, North Carolina. Union officials protested that the men should have been treated as prisoners of war, and eventually an inquiry was made into the events by the House of Representatives; many of the executed soldiers' wives offered testimony which is recorded in those documents.

Collins, Donald E. "Eastern North Carolinians in the Union Army: The First and Second North Carolina Union Volunteer Regiments." http://homepages.rootsweb.com/~ncuv/collins1.htm

Collins, Donald E. "War Crime or Justice? General George Pickett and the Mass Execution of Deserters in Civil War Kinston, North Carolina." http://homepages.rootsweb.com/~ncuv/kinston2.htm

Paris, John. *A Sermon: Preached before Brig.-Gen. Hoke's Brigade, at Kinston, N. C., on the 28th of February, 1864, by Rev. John Paris, Chaplain Fifty-Fourth Regiment N. C. Troops, upon the Death of Twenty-Two Men, Who Had Been Executed in the*

*Presence of the Brigade for the Crime of Desertion.* Greensboro: A. W. Ingold & Co., 1864

QUOTATIONS: Paris, John. "The Deserter's Doom: John Paris, Chaplain 54th Regiment N. C. T. Kinston, North Carolina, February 22nd, 1864." *The North Carolina Presbyterian*, April 13, 1864

### 1865: Mary Eugenia Surratt

Christian Rath was the captain in charge of the execution, and William Coxshall was one of the men assigned to pull posts out from underneath the hinged drops of the gallows, hanging the four condemned; both men wrote accounts of their experiences. Mary Surratt's priest was among those who said she was innocent, and that there was "not enough evidence to hang a cat." "Traitress" is a quotation from the pamphlet by "Amator Justiae," the final couplet is an observation from the *Washington Intelligencer*. The rest of the quotations come from Rath's "Account."

Coxshall, William E. "'One of the Grimmest Events I Ever Participated In': William E. Coxshall and the Execution of the Lincoln Conspirators." *The Lincoln Ledger*, November 1995

QUOTATIONS: Amator Justiae. "Trial of Mrs. Surratt." *Washington Intelligencer*, July 8, 1865

Moore, Guy W. *The Case of Mrs. Surratt.* Norman: University of Oklahoma Press, 1954

Rath, Christian. "Fate of the Lincoln Conspirators: The Account of the Hanging, given by Lieutenant Colonel Christan Rath, the Executioner." *McClure's*, October 1911

Swanson, James L., ed. *Lincoln's Assassins: Their Trial and Execution. An Illustrated History* Santa Fe: Arena Editions, 2001

### 1865: Major Henry Wirz

A Swiss national loyal to the Confederate cause, Wirz was assigned the post at Andersonville in 1864.

Page, James Madison. *The True Story of Andersonville Prison: A Defense of Major Henry Wirz.* New York: The Neale Publishing Company, 1908

Chipman, N. P. *The Tragedy of Andersonville: Trial of Captain Henry Wirz, the Prison Keeper.* San Francisco: N. P. Chipman, 1911

QUOTATIONS: McElroy, John. *This Was Andersonville.* New York: McDowell, Obolensky, Inc., 1957

*The New York Times*

### 1884: George Cooke

Brown, Larry K. *You Are Cordially Invited to Attend My Execution: Untold Stories of Men Legally Executed in Wyoming Territory.* Glendo, Wyoming: High Plains Press, 1997

QUOTATIONS: Beery, Gladys. "He Died Game." *Real West*, October 1983

### 1890: William Kemmler

Kemmler was convicted of murdering his common-law wife, Tillie Ziegler. He used a hatchet and admitted the crime to a neighbor immediately afterward.

QUOTATIONS: Euripides. *Medea*. Trans. Rex Warner. New York: Dover Books
1992
*The New York Times*

### 1895: Michael McDonough

I used Espy's list of executions by name to find that there have been two
McDonoughs executed in the United States; Michael McDonough was
hanged for killing his wife in Ohio in 1895, and John McDonough was
hanged for rape in Pennsylvania in 1786. "Fresh Ohio News" is from the
*Cleveland Gazette*.

QUOTATIONS: *Cleveland Gazette*
*Cleveland Press*

### 1901: Leon Czolgosz

Czolgosz, an aspiring anarchist, shot President McKinley twice at the Pan
American Exposition in Buffalo, New York.

QUOTATIONS: MacDonald, Carlos F. "The Trial, Execution, Autopsy, and
Mental Status of Leon F. Czolgosz." *Journal of Mental Pathology* 1, 1901–1902

### 1916: Juan Sanchez

Sanchez was one of Pancho Villa's Villistas captured in Columbus, New
Mexico.

QUOTATIONS: "Rope and Rope Making." *Encyclopedia Britannica*. New York:
The Encyclopedia Britannica Co., 1929

Johnston, J. A. "Warden J. A. Johnston of San Quentin to Herbert J. McGrath,
sheriff of Grant County, New Mexico, who was preparing to conduct his
first execution." *La Gaceta, El Boletin de Corral de Santa Fe Westerner*, June
1964

### 1924: Gee Jon

Jon was a hired killer executed for the murder of a rival tong member. *Chung
Sai Yat Po* was the Chinese newspaper in San Francisco; the quotation
from the paper was translated as part of Chan's article.

QUOTATIONS: Chan, Loren B. "Example for the Nation: Nevada's Execution
of Gee Jon." *Nevada Historical Society Quarterly 18*. 1975

Dillon, Richard H. *The Hatchet Men: The Story of the Tong Wars in San Francisco's
Chinatown*. New York: Coward-McCann, Inc., 1963

### 1927: Nicola Sacco

Sacco and Vanzetti were Italian immigrants convicted of murder in the
course of a robbery outside Boston. Their imprisonment lasted from 1921
until their executions.

Russell, Francis. *Tragedy in Dedham: the Story of the Sacco and Vanzetti Case*. New
York: McGraw-Hill, 1971

The Boston Athenaeum's collection of Sacco and Vanzetti ephemera

QUOTATIONS: Sacco, Nicola and Bartolomeo Vanzetti. *The Letters of Sacco and
Vanzetti*. Ed. Marion Denman Frankfurter. New York: Viking Press, 1928

### 1927: Bartolomeo Vanzetti

Public attention for Sacco and Vanzetti has continued long after their executions; in 1961 ballistics tests indicated that Sacco's gun was used during the robbery. Most authorities agree that Vanzetti was innocent.

Russell, Francis. *Tragedy in Dedham: the Story of the Sacco and Vanzetti Case.* New York: McGraw-Hill, 1971

The Boston Athenaeum's collection of Sacco and Vanzetti ephemera

QUOTATIONS: Plato. *Plato's Phaedo: translated with introduction and commentary by R. Hackforth.* Cambridge: University Press, 1955

Sacco, Nicola and Bartolomeo Vanzetti. *The Letters of Sacco and Vanzetti.* Ed. Marion Denman Frankfurter. New York: Viking Press, 1928

### 1936: Rainey Bethea

There was no question of Bethea's guilt; he confessed the rape and murder of 70-year-old Elischa Edwards, his bloody prints were found throughout the crime scene, and he was still stained with her blood when he was found. The black community's call for his hanging helped prevent retaliatory lynchings. His execution was the last public hanging in the United States, and was widely documented and discussed in the press.

QUOTATIONS: Ryan, Perry T. *The Last Public Execution in America.* Kentucky: P. T. Ryan, 1992

### 1945: Private Eddie D. Slovik

Slovik spent a lot of time in homes for juvenile offenders before meeting his wife, settling down, and enlisting in the army. No one expected deserters to be executed in 1945; Slovik himself said "They're not executing me because I ran away; they're executing me because of the bread I stole when I was ten."

QUOTATIONS: Huie, William Bradford. *The Execution of Private Slovik: the Hitherto Secret Story of the Only American Soldier Since 1864 to be Shot for Desertion.* New York: Duell, Sloane and Pearce, 1954

### 1946, 1947: Willie Francis

Francis was convicted of murdering a pharmacist in the process of robbing a drugstore.

QUOTATIONS: Miller, Arthur S. *Death by Installments: The Ordeal of Willie Francis.* New York: Greenwood Press, 1988

### 1953: Julius and Ethel Rosenberg

The Rosenbergs were convicted of selling American atomic secrets to the Soviet government. David Greenglass, Ethel Rosenberg's younger brother, was convicted of being in the same spy ring. He offered substantial evidence against the Rosenbergs, and was released after ten years in prison.

Wexley, John. *The Judgment of Julius and Ethel Rosenberg.* New York: Cameron and Kahn, 1955

QUOTATIONS: Rosenberg, Julius and Ethel. *The Rosenberg Letters.* London: Dennis Dobson, 1953

### 1960: Caryl Chessman

Chessman was convicted of kidnapping and rape in 1947. While now it's common for the condemned to be incarcerated for years before their executions, and to spend a great deal of time on appeals, at the time it was unusual. Chessman worked hard to make his case public, and published several books about his life and experiences.

QUOTATIONS: Chessman, Caryl. *Cell 2455, Death Row*. New York: Prentice-Hall, 1954

### 1965: Perry Smith

Smith and Richard Hickock were convicted of murdering the Clutters, a family of four in Holcomb, Kansas. Truman Capote's book about the murders relied on interviews with Smith and Hickock as well as residents of Holcomb; portions first appeared in *The New Yorker*.

QUOTATIONS: Capote, Truman. *In Cold Blood*. New York: Random House, 1965

### 1977: Gary Gilmore

In 1972 the Supreme Court ruled that the death penalty statutes of forty states were unconstitutional. There were no executions in the United States from 1972 to 1977, while the states changed their statutes. In 1976 the court reinstated capital punishment. Gilmore, convicted of murdering two clerks, requested the death penalty; he was the first person executed after the reinstution of the punishment.

QUOTATIONS: Gilmore, Mikal. *Shot in the Heart*. New York: Doubleday, 1994
*The New York Times*

### 1982: Charles Brooks

Brooks was the first black man legally executed in America since 1967. *The Dallas Morning News*: "Officials said the remaining 171 prisoners with death sentences in Texas appeared stunned by Brooks' execution, which capital-penalty opponents warned might spark a 'bloodbath' in Texas and the South."

QUOTATIONS: *The Dallas Morning News*
*The New York Times*

### 1986: Daniel Morris Thomas

Thomas was the leader of the Ski Mask Gang, which authorities said was responsible for a ten-month "rampage against whites" in which several people were beaten, five raped, and two murdered. "A black informant was used to infiltrate the gang. After the gang members' arrests, the informant collected about $7,000 in rewards, including $1,000 from the Ku Klux Klan. The informant died in 1983."

QUOTATIONS: *Miami Herald*

### 1997: Bruce Edwin Callins

Callins shot and killed a man while holding up a topless bar.

QUOTATIONS: Callins' letter to Blackmun is available online:
http://www.nytimes.com/packages/html/national/20040304_BLACKMUN
_FEATURE/

The full text of the ruling in the Callins' case is also available online:
http://www.pbs.org/newshour/bb/law/supreme_court/blackmun/
   blackmun_opinions.html

## 2000: Shaka Sankofa, formerly known as Gary Graham

In *Warden: Prison Life and Death from the Inside Out*, Walls Unit Warden James
   Willett describes Sankofa's execution in detail, including the struggle
   between guards and Sankofa just before the execution. Here he describes
   Sankofa's last statement; lifting his glasses was a signal he used when it
   was time for the executioner to start the injection. "I tell Graham that he
   may make a statement now, if he wishes. He begins by saying that he
   never killed anybody, then speeds up and shouts that we need to stop
   killing black people. Then he goes on for five minutes, which is the time
   limit I gave him last night. He finally stops, and I ask if he's done. He
   starts again, delivering at breakneck speed a long harrangue about racial
   prejudice and injustice. After nearly six more minutes, I sigh, lift my
   glasses from the bridge of my nose, and watch, about thirty seconds later,
   as Graham falls asleep in mid-sentence."
QUOTATIONS: Welch, Mandy and Richard Burr. "The Politics of Finality and
   the Execution of the Innocent: The Case of Gary Graham" *Machinery of
   Death: The Reality of America's Death Penalty Regime*. Ed. David R. Dow and
   Mark Dow. New York: Routledge, 2002
*Houston Chronicle*
*The New York Times*
Gary Graham's last words are available online:
   http://www.tdcj.state.tx.us/stat/grahamgarylast.htm

## 2000: Brian Roberson

Roberson was the 139th person executed during Bush's term as Texas gover-
   nor.
QUOTATIONS: http://web.amnesty.org/library/Index/ENGAMR511132000?
   open&of=ENG-392
*The New York Times*
www.txexecutions.org

## 2000: Oliver Cruz

Raymond Bonner, *New York Times* reporter, interviewed Cruz about his IQ:
   "Mr. Cruz did not appear to know what it meant to be mentally retarded.
   'I'm not retarded,' he said. 'I'm not the kind of person who is going to go
   out and hurt people for the fun of it.'"
QUOTATIONS: *Houston Chronicle*
*The New York Times*

## 2001: Timothy McVeigh

McVeigh and Terry Nichols exploded a truck bomb outside the Alfred P.
   Murrah Federal Building in Oklahoma City in 1995, killing 168 people.
   Nichols is serving a life sentence in prison.
QUOTATIONS: *The New York Times*

**2002: Aileen Wuornos**

Wuornos is considered to be the only female serial killer in American history. Her victims were men who picked her up on Florida highways; Charlize Theron won an Oscar for her portrayal of Wuornos in the film *Monster*.

*Monster*. Dir. Patty Jenkins. Perf. Charlize Theron, Christina Ricci. NewMarket Films, 2003

*Aileen Wuornos: The Selling of a Serial Killer*. Dir. Nick Broomfield. 1992

QUOTATIONS: *Aileen: Life and Death of a Serial Killer*. Dir. Nick Broomfield. 2003

**2003: Paul Hill**

Hill shot and killed James Barrett, a security guard, and Dr. John Britton, one of the nine "dead babykilling abortionists" listed on The Army of God website. Other websites that were helpful in understanding Paul Hill included those of A Mighty Wind, Free Jesus, and A Voice in the Wilderness.

*The Boston Globe*

**2005: Michael Ross**

Newspaper articles about Ross and Ross' own writings are collected at the website of the Canadian Coalition Against the Death Penalty, www.ccdap.org. *The Times* provided information on the psychiatrists' diagnoses, the *Globe* covered the protests, and the *Hartford Courant* had the most thorough coverage of the victims' families' responses to the execution.

QUOTATIONS: www.ccdap.org

*The New York Times*

*The Boston Globe*

*The Hartford Courant*

CPSIA information can be obtained at www.ICGtesting.com
Printed in the USA
LVOW11s1818210415

435475LV00006B/887/P